I0866883

BEGINNER LEVEL

Sensory Baby Toys

15 HANDMADE CROCHET CUTIES

LEISURE ARTS, INC. • Maumelle, Arkansas

CONTENTS

BEEHIVE BABY SET

EASY

Finished Measurements:

Mobile - 20" (51 cm) tall and 6" (15 cm) wide

Garland - 42" (106.5 cm) long

Stroller Toy - 13" (33 cm) long (with Clip)

Rattle - 6" (15 cm) long and 6" (15 cm) wide

Teething Toy - 4" x 5½" (10 cm x 14 cm)

SHOPPING LIST

Yarn (Light Weight) LIGHT 3

[5 ounces, 362 yards (140 grams, 331 meters) per skein]:

- ☐ Gold - 1 skein
- ☐ Grey - 1 skein
- ☐ Brown - 1 skein
- ☐ White - 1 skein
- ☐ Yellow - 1 skein
- ☐ Pink and Black - small amount

Crochet Hook

- ☐ Size D (3.25 mm)

Additional Supplies

- ☐ Stitch marker
- ☐ Ring for Mobile
- ☐ 2¼" (5.5 cm) Wooden ring - 2
- ☐ 1¼" (3.25 cm) Wooden ring - 1
- ☐ Badge clips or alligator clips
- ☐ Large bell or plastic ball cat toy (for Rattle)
- ☐ Wooden geometric beads
- ☐ Yarn needle
- ☐ Polyester fiberfill
- ☐ Strong matching thread (double-strand for assembly)

STITCH GUIDE

SINGLE CROCHET 2 TOGETHER

(abbreviated sc2tog)

Pull up a loop in each of next 2 sc, YO and draw through all 3 loops on hook **(counts as one sc)**.

MOBILE

Beehive

Rnd 1 (Wrong side)**:** With Gold, ch 2, 8 sc in second ch from hook; place marker to indicate the beginning of the rnd ***(see Markers, page 57)***.

Note: Work in Front Loops Only throughout Beehive ***(Fig. 3, page 59)***.

Rnd 2: 2 Hdc in each sc around: 16 hdc.

Rnd 3: (2 Hdc in next hdc, hdc in next hdc) around: 24 hdc.

Rnd 4: (2 Hdc in next hdc, hdc in next 2 hdc) around: 32 hdc.

Rnd 5: (2 Hdc in next hdc, hdc in next 3 hdc) around: 40 hdc.

Rnd 6: (2 Hdc in next hdc, hdc in next 4 hdc) around: 48 hdc.

Rnd 7: (2 Hdc in next hdc, hdc in next 5 hdc) around: 56 hdc.

Rnd 8: (2 Hdc in next hdc, hdc in next 6 hdc) around: 64 hdc.

Rnd 9: (2 Hdc in next hdc, hdc in next 7 hdc) around: 72 hdc.

Rnd 10: (2 Hdc in next hdc, hdc in next 8 hdc) around: 80 hdc.

Rnds 11-25: Hdc in each hdc around.

Rnd 26: Sc in each hdc around; slip st in **both** loops of next sc, finish off leaving a long end for sewing.

Turn Beehive inside out, so that the ridges from the loops show. Stuff Beehive firmly.

BASE

Rnd 1 (Right side)**:** With Gold, ch 2, 6 sc in second ch from hook; place marker to indicate the beginning of the rnd.

Rnd 2: 2 Sc in each sc around: 12 sc.

Rnd 3: (2 Sc in next sc, sc in next sc) around: 18 sc.

Rnd 4: (2 Sc in next sc, sc in next 2 sc) around: 24 sc.

Rnd 5: (2 Sc in next sc, sc in next 3 sc) around: 30 sc.

Rnd 6: (2 Sc in next sc, sc in next 4 sc) around: 36 sc.

Rnd 7: (2 Sc in next sc, sc in next 5 sc) around: 42 sc.

Rnd 8: (2 Sc in next sc, sc in next 6 sc) around: 48 sc.

Rnd 9: (2 Sc in next sc, sc in next 7 sc) around: 54 sc.

Rnd 10: (2 Sc in next sc, sc in next 8 sc) around: 60 sc.

Rnd 11: (2 Sc in next sc, sc in next 9 sc) around: 66 sc.

Rnd 12: (2 Sc in next sc, sc in next 10 sc) around: 72 sc.

Rnd 13: (2 Sc in next sc, sc in next 11 sc) around: 78 sc.

Rnd 14: (2 Sc in next sc, sc in next 38 sc) twice; slip st in next sc, finish off: 80 sc.

With **wrong** side of Base against bottom of stuffed Beehive, using the long end from the Beehive and working through **both** loops on **both** pieces, whipstitch Beehive closed *(Fig. 6, page 60)*.

HOLE

Row 1 (Right side)**:** With Brown, ch 2, 4 sc in second ch from hook.

Row 2: Ch 1, turn; 2 sc in first sc, 2 hdc in each of next 2 sc, 2 sc in last sc: 8 sts.

Row 3: Ch 1, turn; sc in first sc, 2 sc in next sc, hdc in next hdc, 2 hdc in each of next 2 hdc, hdc in next hdc, 2 sc in next sc, sc in last sc: 12 sts.

Row 4: Ch 1, turn; sc in first 2 sc, 2 sc in next sc, hdc in next 2 hdc, 2 hdc in each of next 2 hdc, hdc in next 2 hdc, 2 sc in next sc, sc in last 2 sc: 16 sts.

Row 5: Ch 1, turn; sc in first 3 sc, 2 sc in next sc, hdc in next 3 hdc, 2 hdc in each of next 2 hdc, hdc in next 3 hdc, 2 sc in next sc, sc in last 3 sc: 20 sts.

Row 6: Ch 1, turn; sc in first 4 sc, 2 sc in next sc, hdc in next 4 hdc, 2 hdc in each of next 2 hdc, hdc in next 4 hdc, 2 sc in next sc, sc in last 4 sc: 24 sts.

Row 7: Ch 1, turn; sc in first 5 sc, 2 sc in next sc, hdc in next 5 hdc, 2 hdc in each of next 2 hdc, hdc in next 5 hdc, 2 sc in next sc, sc in last 5 sc: 28 sts.

Finish off leaving a long end for sewing.

LARGE FLOWER (Make 2)

Rnd 1 (Right side)**:** With Yellow, ch 3, 6 hdc in third ch from hook changing to White in last hdc ***(Fig. 4b, page 59)***; place marker to indicate the beginning of the rnd: 6 hdc.

Rnd 2: (Slip st, 3 hdc) in each hdc around; slip st in first slip st, finish off.

SMALL FLOWER (Make 4)

Rnd 1 (Right side)**:** With Yellow, ch 2, 6 sc in second ch from hook changing to White in last sc made ***(Fig. 4a, page 59)***; place marker to indicate the beginning of the rnd.

Rnd 2: (Slip st, 2 hdc) in each sc around; slip st in first slip st, finish off.

Small Bee (Make 4)

HEAD AND BODY

Rnd 1 (Right side)**:** With Grey, ch 2, 6 sc in second ch from hook; place marker to indicate the beginning of the rnd.

Rnd 2: 2 Sc in each sc around: 12 sc.

Rnd 3: (2 Sc in next sc, sc in next sc) around: 18 sc.

Rnds 4-7: Sc in each sc around stuffing Head firmly as you work.

Rnd 8: Sc2tog around changing to Yellow in last sc made, drop Grey to wrong side: 9 sc.

Rnd 9: 2 Sc in each sc around: 18 sc.

Rnd 10: Sc in each sc around changing to Grey in last sc made, drop Yellow to wrong side.

Rnds 11 and 12: Sc in each sc around, changing to Yellow in last sc of Rnd 12, drop Grey to wrong side.

Rnds 13 and 14: Sc in each sc around, changing to Grey in last sc of Rnd 14, cut Yellow.

Rnd 15: Sc in each sc around stuffing piece firmly.

Rnd 16: Sc2tog around: 9 sc.

Rnd 17: Sc in each sc around.

Rnd 18: (Sc2tog, sc in next sc) 3 times: 6 sc.

Rnd 19: Sc in each sc around; slip st in next sc, finish off leaving a long end for sewing.

Stuff piece firmly. Thread yarn needle with long end and weave through remaining 6 sts ***(Fig. 5, page 60)***; pull **tightly** to close and secure end.

WINGS (Make 2)
With White, ch 7.

Row 1: Sc in second ch from hook and in next 2 chs, hdc in next 2 chs, 6 hdc in last ch; working in free loops on opposite side of ch ***(Fig. 2, page 59)***, hdc in next 2 chs, sc in next 3 chs; finish off leaving a long end for sewing.

ASSEMBLY

See Embroidery Stitches, pages 60 & 61.

Assemble 3 "Flying" Bees as follows referring to photo as a guide:

- Sew 2 Wings to back, across Rnds 10 and 11.
- Add Black French knot eyes between Rnds 2 and 3.
- Embroider two ½" (12 mm) long antennae on the top of the Head. With Pink, embroider a "V" for the mouth.

Assemble One "Standing" Bee as follows referring to photo as a guide:

- Sew 2 Wings to back, across Rnds 9 and 10.
- On opposite side from Wings, add Black French knot eyes on Rnd 4, spacing them 4 sts apart.
- Embroider two ½" (12 mm) long antennae on top of the Head.
- With Pink, embroider a "V" for the mouth on Rnd 4.

Finishing

Using photo as a guide for placement:

- With long end, sew Hole to Beehive, aligning straight edge of Hole with edge of Base.
- With strong thread, sew a small wood ring, 1" (2.5 cm) from the top of the beehive.
- Sew Flowers to Beehive.
- With strong thread, sew the "standing" bee 2" (5 cm) from the center of the Base.
- Sew "flying" bees evenly around edge of Base, sewing one with strong thead hanging 7" (18 cm) from Beehive, one hanging 9" (23 cm) from Beehive, and the last one hanging 11" (28 cm) from Beehive.

GARLAND

Small Beehive (Make 2)

Rnd 1 (Wrong side)**:** With Gold, ch 2, 8 sc in second ch from hook; place marker to indicate the beginning of the rnd.

Note: Work in Front Loops Only throughout.

Rnd 2: 2 Hdc in each sc around: 16 hdc.

Rnd 3: (2 Hdc in next hdc, hdc in next hdc) around: 24 hdc.

Rnd 4: (2 Hdc in next hdc, hdc in next 2 hdc) around: 32 hdc.

Rnds 5-11: Hdc in each hdc around.

Rnd 12: Sc in each hdc around; slip st in both loops of next sc, finish off leaving a long end for sewing.

HOLE

Row 1: With Brown, ch 2, 4 sc in second ch from hook.

Row 2: Ch 1, turn: 2 sc in each sc across: 8 sc.

Row 3: Ch 1, turn; sc in first 2 sc, 2 hdc in each of next 4 sc, sc in last 2 sc: 12 sts.

Row 4: Ch 1, turn; sc in first 3 sts, hdc in next hdc, 2 hdc in each of next 4 hdc, hdc in next hdc, sc in last 3 sts; finish off leaving a long end for sewing: 16 sts.

SMALL FLOWER (Make 3)

Rnd 1 (Right side)**:** With Yellow, ch 2, 6 sc in second ch from hook changing to White in last sc made; place marker to indicate the beginning of the rnd.

Rnd 2: (Slip st, 2 hdc) in each sc around; slip st in first slip st, finish off.

ASSEMBLY

Turn Beehive inside out, so that the ridges from the loops show. Stuff Beehive firmly. Flatten bottom of Beehive; with long end, sew bottom closed. Sew Hole to center bottom of Beehive. Sew Flowers to front of Beehive.

Large Crochet Bead

(Make 2 **each** with Gold and White & one **each** with Yellow and Grey)

Rnd 1 (Right side)**:** With color indicated, ch 2, 6 sc in second ch from hook; place marker to indicate the beginning of the rnd.

Rnd 2: 2 Sc in each sc around: 12 sc.

Rnd 3: (2 Sc in next sc, sc in next sc) around: 18 sc.

Rnds 4-7: Sc in each sc around, stuffing Bead as you work.

Rnd 8: (Sc2tog, sc in next sc) around: 12 sc.

Rnd 9: Sc2tog around; finish off leaving a long end for sewing: 6 sts.

Stuff piece firmly. Thread yarn needle with long end and weave through remaining 6 sts; pull **tightly** to close and secure end.

Small Crochet Bead (Make 2 **each** with Grey, Gold, White & Yellow)

Rnd 1 (Right side)**:** With color indicated, ch 2, 6 sc in second ch from hook; place marker to indicate the beginning of the rnd.

Rnd 2: 2 Sc in each sc around: 12 sc.

Rnds 3-5: Sc in each sc around, stuffing Bead as you work.

Rnd 6: Sc2tog around; slip st in next sc, finish off leaving a long end for sewing: 6 sts.

Stuff piece firmly. Thread yarn needle with long end and weave through remaining 6 sts; pull **tightly** to close and secure end.

Small Bee (Make 2)

Work same as Mobile Small Bee and assemble them as 2 "standing" Bees.

Bear

Work same as Bear, page 17.

Finishing

Using strong thread, make a 5" (12.5 cm) loop on one end and thread the pieces from **right** to **left** in the following order:

Large Gold bead, small Grey bead, 1 geometric wood bead, small beehive, large White bead, 1 geometric wood bead, small Yellow bead, small Bee, small Gold bead, large Grey bead, 1 geometric wood bead, small White bead, Bear, small Yellow bead, 1 geometric wood bead, large Gold bead, small White bead, small Bee, small Gold bead, 1 geometric wood bead, large Yellow bead, small Beehive, 1 geometric wood bead, small Grey bead, large White bead.

Make a 5" (12.5 cm) loop with strong thread at left end.

STROLLER TOY

Small Beehive

Rnd 1 (Right side)**:** With Gold, ch 2, 8 sc in second ch from hook; place marker to indicate the beginning of the rnd.

Note: Work in Front Loops Only throughout.

Rnd 2: 2 Hdc in each sc around: 16 hdc.

Rnd 3: (2 Hdc in next hdc, hdc in next hdc) around: 24 hdc.

Rnd 4: (2 Hdc in next hdc, hdc in each of the next 2 hdc) around: 32 hdc.

Rnds 5-11: Hdc in each hdc around: 32 hdc.

Rnd 12: Sc in each sc around; slip st in both loops of next sc, finish off leaving a long end for sewing: 32 sc.

HOLE

Row 1 (Right side)**:** With Brown, ch 2, 4 sc in second ch from hook.

Row 2: Ch 1, turn; 2 sc in each sc across: 8 sc.

Row 3: Ch 1, turn; sc in first 2 sc, 2 hdc in each of next 4 sc, sc in last 2 sc: 12 sts.

Row 4: Ch 1, turn; sc in first 3 sts, hdc in next hdc, 2 hdc in each of next 4 hdc, hdc in next hdc, sc in last 3 sts; finish off leaving a long end for sewing: 16 sts.

SMALL FLOWER (Make 2)

Rnd 1 (Right side)**:** With Yellow, ch 2, 6 sc in second ch from hook changing to White in last sc made; place marker to indicate the beginning of the rnd.

Rnd 2: (Slip st, 2 hdc) in each sc around; slip st in first slip st, finish off.

ASSEMBLY

Turn Beehive inside out, so that the ridges from the loops show. Stuff Beehive firmly. Flatten bottom of Beehive; with long end, sew bottom closed. Sew Hole to bottom center of Beehive. Sew Small Flowers to front of Beehive.

Large Crochet Bead

Rnd 1 (Right side)**:** With Grey, ch 2, 6 sc in second ch from hook; place marker to indicate the beginning of the rnd.

Rnd 2: 2 Sc in each sc around: 12 sc.

Rnd 3: (2 Sc in next sc, sc in next sc) around: 18 sc.

Rnds 4-7: Sc in each sc around.

Rnd 8: (Sc2tog, sc in next sc) around, stuffing Bead as you work: 12 sc.

Rnd 9: Sc2tog around; finish off leaving a long end for sewing: 6 sts.

Stuff piece firmly. Thread yarn needle with long end and weave through remaining 6 sts; pull **tightly** to close and secure end.

Small Crochet Bead

Rnd 1 (Right side)**:** With Yellow, ch 2, 6 sc in second ch from hook; place marker to indicate the beginning of the rnd.

Rnd 2: 2 Sc in each sc around: 12 sc.

Rnds 3-5: Sc in each sc around, stuffing Bead as you work.

Rnd 6: Sc2tog around; slip st in next sc, finish off leaving a long end for sewing: 6 sts.

Stuff piece firmly. Thread yarn needle with long end and weave through remaining 6 sts; pull **tightly** to close and secure end.

Bear

HEAD & BODY

Rnd 1 (Right side)**:** With Brown and beginning at top of Head, ch 2, 6 sc in second ch from hook; place marker to indicate the beginning of the rnd.

Rnd 2: 2 Sc in each sc around: 12 sc.

Rnd 3: (2 Sc in next sc, sc in next sc) around: 18 sc.

Rnd 4: (2 Sc in next sc, sc in next 2 sc) around: 24 sc.

Rnd 5: (2 Sc in next sc, sc in next 3 sc) around: 30 sc.

Rnds 6-24: Sc in each sc around.

Finish off leaving a long end for sewing.

MUZZLE

Rnd 1: With Brown, ch 2, 8 sc in second ch from hook; place marker to indicate the beginning of the rnd.

Rnd 2: 2 Sc in each of next 2 sc, hdc in next 6 sc: 10 sc.

Rnd 3: Sc in next sc, 2 sc in next 2 sc, sc in next sc, hdc in next 6 hdc: 12 sc.

Rnd 4: Sc in next 6 sc, hdc in next 6 hdc; finish off leaving a long end for sewing.

EAR (Make 2)
Row 1 (Right side)**:** With Brown, ch 2, 3 sc in second ch from hook.

Row 2: Ch 1, turn; 2 sc in first sc, 2 hdc in next sc, 2 sc in last sc: 6 sts.

Row 3: Ch 1, turn; sc in first sc, 2 sc in next sc, 2 hdc in each of next 2 hdc, 2 sc in next sc, sc in last sc; finish off leaving a long end for sewing.

ARM/LEG (Make 4)
Rnd 1 (Right side)**:** With Brown, ch 2, 8 sc in second ch from hook; place marker to indicate the beginning of the rnd.

Rnds 2-6: Sc in each sc around.

Finish off leaving a long end for sewing.

ASSEMBLY
Stuff Body. Flatten bottom of Bear; with long end, sew bottom closed. Stuff the Muzzle and center at top of Body with the hdc sts as the top of the Muzzle. With long end, sew Muzzle to Head. With a scrap of Black yarn, embroider the eyes, nose and mouth. Sew Ears to the top of the Head with long ends. Stuff the Arms and Legs lightly. Sew the Legs to the bottom sewn edge of the Body. Arrange and sew Arms to each side of Body.

Finishing

To make the stroller toy, use strong thread and secure it to the clip (badge or alligator); then thread the pieces from top to bottom in the following order:
Large Grey bead, 1 geometric wood bead, small Beehive, small Yellow bead, 1 geometric wood bead, then attach the Bear securely at the bottom.

RATTLE

Bee

HEAD AND BODY

Rnd 1 (Right side)**:** With Grey, ch 2, 6 sc in second ch from hook; place marker to indicate the beginning of the rnd.

Rnd 2: 2 Sc in each sc around: 12 sc.

Rnd 3: (2 Sc in next sc, sc in next sc) around: 18 sc.

Rnd 4: (2 Sc in next sc, sc in next 2 sc) around: 24 sc.

Rnd 5: (2 Sc in next sc, sc in next 3 sc) around: 30 sc.

Rnd 6: (2 Sc in next sc, sc in next 4 sc) around: 36 sc.

Rnds 7-12: Sc in each sc around, stuffing Head as you work.

Rnd 13: (Sc2tog, sc in next 4 sc) around: 30 sc.

Rnd 14: (Sc2tog, sc in next 3 sc) around: 24 sc.

Rnd 15: (Sc2tog, sc in next 2 sc) around, stuffing Head firmly as you work, insert large bell or cat toy in center: 18 sc.

Rnd 16: (Sc2tog, sc in next sc) around, changing to Yellow in last sc, drop Grey to wrong side: 12 sc.

Rnd 17: Sc in each sc around.

Rnd 18: 2 Sc in each sc around: 24 sc.

Rnd 19: Sc in each sc around, changing to Grey in last sc, drop Yellow to wrong side.

Rnds 20-22: Sc in each sc around, changing to Yellow in last sc of Rnd 22, drop Grey to wrong side.

Rnds 23-25: Sc in each sc around, changing to Grey in last sc of Rnd 25, drop Yellow to wrong side.

Rnds 26-28: Sc in each sc around, changing to Yellow in last sc of Rnd 28, drop Grey to wrong side.

Rnds 29-31: Sc in each sc around, changing to Grey in last sc of Rnd 31, cut Yellow.

Rnd 32: Sc in each sc around, stuffing Body firmly as you work.

Rnd 33: Sc2tog around: 12 sc.

Rnd 34: Sc in each sc around.

Rnd 35: (Sc2tog, sc in next sc) around, stuffing as you work: 8 sc.

Rnd 36: Sc in each sc around.

Rnd 37: Sc2tog around: 4 sc.

Rnd 38: Sc in each sc around; slip st in next sc, finish off leaving a long end for sewing.

Stuff piece firmly. Thread yarn needle with long end and weave through remaining 4 sts; pull **tightly** to close and secure end.

Wing Cover (Make 2)

With White, ch 13.

Row 1: Sc in second ch from hook and in each ch across: 12 sc.

Rows 2-6: Ch 1, turn; sc in each sc across: 12 sc.

Finish off leaving a long end for sewing.

Wrap Wing Cover around 2¼" (5.5 cm) wooden ring; using long end, sew top of last row to base of beginning ch.

Finishing

Using photo as a guide for placement:

- Sew rings to each side of Head.
- With Black, add French knot eyes, and add 1" (2.5 cm) antennae.
- With Pink, embroider the mouth.

TEETHING TOY

Large Crochet Bead

(Make one **each** with Gold and White)

Rnd 1 (Right side)**:** With color indicated, ch 2, 6 sc in second ch from hook; place marker to indicate the beginning of the rnd.

Rnd 2: 2 Sc in each sc around: 12 sc.

Rnd 3: (2 Sc in next sc, sc in next sc) around: 18 sc.

Rnds 4-7: Sc in each sc around, stuffing Bead as you work.

Rnd 8: (Sc2tog, sc in next sc) around: 12 sc.

Rnd 9: Sc2tog around; slip st in next sc, finish off leaving a long end for sewing: 6 sts.

Stuff piece firmly. Thread yarn needle with long end and weave through remaining 6 sts; pull **tightly** to close and secure end.

Small Crochet Bead (Make one **each** with Gold, White and Grey)

Rnd 1 (Right side)**:** With color indicated, ch 2, 6 sc in second ch from hook; place marker to indicate the beginning of the rnd.

Rnd 2: 2 Sc in each sc around: 12 sc.

Rnds 3-5: Sc in each sc around, stuffing Bead as you work.

Rnd 6: Sc2tog around; slip st in next sc, finish off leaving a long end for sewing: 6 sts.

Stuff piece firmly. Thread yarn needle with long end and weave through remaining 6 sts; pull **tightly** to close and secure end.

Small Bee

Work same as Mobile Small Bee, page 10, and assemble as a "standing" Bee.

Finishing

Using strong thread and photo as a guide for placement, insert thread thru each piece in the following order:

Small Bee, small White bead, 1 geometric wood bead, large Gold bead, 1 geometric wood bead, small Grey bead, 1 geometric wood bead, large White bead, 1 geometric wood bead, and small Gold bead.

Securely connect the last small Gold bead to the Bee at the beginning.

Designs by Amy Gaines.

BABY
BABY

BUNNY BABY SET

TREE

EASY

Finished Measurements:

Mobile - 24" (61 cm)

Garland - 45" (114.5 cm) long

Stroller Toy - 19" (48.5 cm) long (with Clip)

Rattle - 7½" (19 cm) high

Teething Toy - 5" wide x 3" high (12.5 cm x 7.5 cm)

SHOPPING LIST

Yarn (Medium Weight) 4

[3.5 ounces, 170 yards (100 grams, 156 meters) per skein]:

- ☐ White - 1 skein
- ☐ Medium Brown - 1 skein
- ☐ Dk Brown - 1 skein
- ☐ Green - 1 skein
- ☐ Grey - 1 skein
- ☐ Lt Grey - 1 skein
- ☐ Pink and Black - small amount

Crochet Hook

- ☐ Size G (4 mm) (for Mobile, Garland & Stroller Toy) Size D (3.25 mm) **and** Size F (3.75 mm) (for Rattle & Teething Toy)

Additional Supplies

- ☐ Stitch marker
- ☐ 1½" (4 cm) Plastic ring
- ☐ Wooden Beads- Large and small
- ☐ Badge clip or alligator clip - 2
- ☐ Large bell or plastic ball cat toy (for Rattle)
- ☐ Alphabet beads
- ☐ Yarn needle
- ☐ Polyfill fiberfill
- ☐ Strong matching thread (double-strand for assembly)

STITCH GUIDE

TREBLE CROCHET ***(abbreviated tr)***

YO twice, insert hook in sp indicated, YO and pull up a loop (4 loops on hook), (YO and draw through 2 loops on hook) 3 times.

SINGLE CROCHET 2 TOGETHER ***(abbreviated sc2tog)***

Pull up a loop in each of next 2 sc, YO and draw through all 3 loops on hook **(counts as one sc)**.

MOBILE

Mountain

Rnd 1 (Right side)**:** With Grey, ch 3, 6 hdc in third ch from hook; place marker to indicate the beginning of the rnd *(see Markers, page 57)*.

Rnd 2: Hdc in each hdc around.

Rnd 3: (2 Hdc in next hdc, hdc in next hdc) around: 9 hdc.

Rnd 4: (2 Hdc in next hdc, hdc in next 2 hdc) around: 12 hdc.

Rnd 5: (2 Hdc in next hdc, hdc in next 3 hdc) around: 15 hdc.

Rnd 6: (2 Hdc in next hdc, hdc in next 4 hdc) around: 18 hdc.

Rnd 7: (2 Hdc in next hdc, hdc in next 5 hdc) around: 21 hdc.

Rnd 8: (2 Hdc in next hdc, hdc in next 6 hdc) around: 24 hdc.

Rnd 9: (2 Hdc in next hdc, hdc in next 7 hdc) around: 27 hdc.

Rnd 10: (2 Hdc in next hdc, hdc in next 8 hdc) around: 30 hdc.

Rnd 11: (2 Hdc in next hdc, hdc in next 9 hdc) around: 33 hdc.

Rnd 12: (2 Hdc in next hdc, hdc in next 10 hdc) around: 36 hdc.

Rnd 13: (2 Hdc in next hdc, hdc in next 11 hdc) around: 39 hdc.

Rnd 14: (2 Hdc in next hdc, hdc in next 12 hdc) around: 42 hdc.

Rnd 15: (2 Hdc in next hdc, hdc in next 13 hdc) around: 45 hdc.

Rnd 16: (2 Hdc in next hdc, hdc in next 14 hdc) around: 48 hdc.

Rnd 17: (2 Hdc in next hdc, hdc in next 15 hdc) around: 51 hdc.

Rnd 18: (2 Hdc in next hdc, hdc in next 16 hdc) around: 54 hdc.

Rnd 19: (2 Hdc in next hdc, hdc in next 17 hdc) around: 57 hdc.

Rnd 20: (2 Hdc in next hdc, hdc in next 18 hdc) around; finish off leaving a long end for sewing: 60 hdc.

Stuff Mountain firmly with polyester fiberfill.

BASE

Rnd 1 (Right side)**:** With Grey, ch 2, 6 sc in second ch from hook; place marker to indicate the beginning of the rnd.

Rnd 2: 2 Sc in each sc around: 12 sc.

Rnd 3: (2 Sc in next sc, sc in next sc) around: 18 sc.

Rnd 4: (2 Sc in next sc, sc in next 2 sc) around: 24 sc.

Rnd 5: (2 Sc in next sc, sc in next 3 sc) around: 30 sc.

Rnd 6: (2 Sc in next sc, sc in next 4 sc) around: 36 sc.

Rnd 7: (2 Sc in next sc, sc in next 5 sc) around: 42 sc.

Rnd 8: (2 Sc in next sc, sc in next 6 sc) around: 48 sc.

Rnd 9: (2 Sc in next sc, sc in next 7 sc) around: 54 sc.

Rnd 10: (2 Sc in next sc, sc in next 8 sc) around; slip st in next sc, finish off: 60 sc.

With **wrong** side of Base against the bottom of the stuffed Mountain, and working through **both** loops on **both** pieces, whipstitch pieces together using the long end from the Mountain ***(Fig. 6, page 60)***.

SNOW CAP

Rnd 1 (Right side)**:** With White, ch 2, 6 sc in second ch from hook; place a marker to indicate the beginning of the rnd.

Rnd 2: Sc in each sc around.

Rnd 3: (2 Sc in next sc, sc in next sc) around: 9 sc.

Rnd 4: (2 Sc in next sc, sc in next 2 sc) around: 12 sc.

Rnd 5: (2 Sc in next sc, sc in next 3 sc) around: 15 sc.

Rnd 6: (2 Sc in next sc, sc in next 4 sc) around: 18 sc.

Rnd 7: 2 Sc in next sc, sc in next 5 sc, 2 hdc in next sc, hdc in next 5 sc, 2 sc in next sc, sc in next 5 sc: 21 sts.

Rnd 8: 2 Sc in next sc, sc in next 6 sc, 2 hdc in next hdc, hdc in next 6 hdc, 2 sc in next sc, sc in next 6 sc: 24 sts.

Rnd 9: 2 Sc in next sc, sc in next 7 sc, 2 hdc in next hdc, hdc in next 7 hdc, 2 sc in next sc, sc in next 7 sc: 27 sts.

Rnd 10: 2 Sc in next sc, sc in next 8 sc, 2 hdc in next hdc, hdc in next 8 hdc, 2 sc in the next sc, sc in next 8 sc: 30 sts.

Rnd 11: 2 Sc in next sc, sc in next 9 sc, 2 hdc in next hdc, hdc in next 9 hdc, 2 sc in next sc, sc in next 9 sc: 33 sts.

Rnd 12: Sc in the next 4 sc, hdc in next sc, 2 hdc in next sc, hdc in next sc, sc in next 6 sts, hdc in next 2 hdc, 2 dc in next hdc, hdc in next 4 hdc, sc in next 4 sts, hdc in next 2 sc, 2 hdc in next sc, hdc in next 2 sc, sc in next 4 sc: 36 sts.

Rnd 13: Sc in the next 5 sts, hdc in next hdc, 2 hdc in next hdc, hdc in next hdc, sc in next 7 sts, hdc in the next 2 sts, 2 dc in next dc, hdc in next 4 hdc, sc in each of next 5 sts, hdc in next 2 hdc, 2 hdc in next hdc, hdc in next 2 hdc, sc in next 4 sc.

Finish off leaving a long end for sewing.

ASSEMBLY

Arrange the Snow Cap on the top of the Mountain, and using the long end, sew to Mountain.

Oak Leaf

With Green, ch 12.

Row 1 (Right side)**:** Sc in second ch from hook and in next 9 chs, 6 sc in last ch; working in free loops on opposite side of ch ***(Fig. 2, page 59)***, sc in next 10 chs: 26 sc.

Row 2: Ch 1, turn; sc in first sc, ★ hdc in next sc, (dc, ch 3, slip st) in next sc, slip st in next sc, sc in next sc; repeat from ★ 2 times **more**, 2 hdc in same st as last sc, (2 hdc, sc) in next sc, † slip st in next sc, (slip st, ch 3, dc) in next sc, hdc in next sc, sc in next sc †; repeat from † to † 2 times **more**, slip st in first sc, ch 4 (for stem); finish off.

Acorn

Rnd 1 (Right side)**:** With Medium Brown, ch 2, 3 sc in second ch from hook; place marker to indicate the beginning of the rnd.

Rnd 2: 2 Sc in each sc around: 6 sc.

Rnd 3: 2 Sc in each sc around: 12 sc.

Rnd 4: (2 Sc in next sc, sc in next sc) around: 18 sc.

Rnds 5-11: Sc in each sc around.

Rnd 12: (Sc2tog, sc in next sc) around, stuffing piece as you work: 12 sc.

Rnd 13: Sc2tog around; slip st in next sc, finish off leaving a long end for sewing: 6 sts.

Stuff piece firmly. Thread yarn needle with long end and weave through remaining 6 sts ***(Fig. 5, page 60)***; pull **tightly** to close and secure end.

ACORN CAP

Rnd 1 (Right side)**:** With Dk Brown, ch 2, 10 sc in second ch from hook; place marker to indicate the beginning of the rnd.

Rnd 2: 2 Sc in each sc around: 20 sc.

Rnd 3: (2 Sc in next sc, sc in next sc) around: 30 sc.

Rnd 4: Sc in each sc around.

Rnd 5: (Sc2tog, sc in next sc) around; slip st in next sc, finish off leaving a long end for sewing: 20 sc.

ASSEMBLY

Arrange Acorn Cap on top of Acorn and with long end, sew Cap to Acorn. Make a ½" (12 mm) loop on the top of the Cap to form the stem.

Standing Bunny

HEAD & BODY

Rnd 1 (Right side)**:** With Medium Brown and beginning at top of Head, ch 2, 6 sc in second ch from hook; place marker to indicate the beginning of the rnd.

Rnd 2: 2 Sc in each sc around: 12 sc.

Rnd 3: (2 Sc in next sc, sc in next sc) around: 18 sc.

Rnds 4-16: Sc in each sc around.

Slip st in next sc, finish off leaving a long end for sewing.

With Black and using satin stitch ***(Fig. 9, page 61)***, add eyes. With Pink and using straight stitch ***(Fig. 10, page 61)***, add Nose.
Stuff Head & Body; flatten bottom of Bunny, and using long end, sew Rnd 16 together.

ARM (Make 2)

Rnd 1 (Right side)**:** With Medium Brown, ch 2, 6 sc in second ch from hook; place marker to indicate the beginning of the rnd.

Rnds 2-5: Sc in each sc around.

Slip st in next sc, finish off leaving a long end for sewing.

Stuff Arms lightly with polyester fiberfill and, with long end, sew to Body.

LEG (Make 2)

Rnd 1 (Right side)**:** With Medium Brown, ch 2, 6 sc in second ch from hook; place marker to indicate the beginning of the rnd.

Rnds 2-4: Sc in each sc around.

Slip st in next sc, finish off leaving a long end for sewing.

Stuff Legs lightly with polyester fiberfill and, with long end, sew to bottom of Body.

EAR (Make 2)
With Medium Brown, ch 6.

Row 1 (Right side)**:** Sc in second ch from hook, hdc in next 2 chs, sc in next ch, (sc, ch 2, sc) in last ch; working in free loops on opposite side of ch, sc in next ch, hdc in next 2 chs, sc in next ch; finish off leaving a long end for sewing.

With long end, sew Ears to top of Head.

TAIL
Rnd 1 (Right side)**:** With White, ch 2, 8 sc in second ch from hook; place marker to indicate the beginning of the rnd.

Rnds 2 and 3: Sc in each sc around, stuffing piece as you work.

Rnd 4: Sc2tog around; slip st in next sc, finish off leaving a long end for sewing: 4 sts.

Stuff Tail firmly. Thread yarn needle with long end and weave through remaining 4 sts; pull **tightly** to close and secure end; then sew Tail to the back of the Body.

Laying Down Bunny

(Make one White Bunny with a Lt Grey Tail and one Lt Grey Bunny with a White Tail)

BODY
With color indicated, ch 11.

Row 1: Sc in second ch from hook and in each ch across: 10 sc.

Rows 2-16: Ch 1, turn; sc in each sc across.

Finish off leaving a long end for sewing.

Fold piece in half lengthwise. Matching free loops of beginning ch at base of sts on Row 1 to top of sts on Row 16, sew bottom closed with long end, then sew end of rows together for side. Stuff Body with polyester fiberfill and sew remaining side seam with matching color (Body makes a stuffed rectangle).

HEAD
Rnd 1 (Right side)**:** With color indicated, ch 2, 6 sc in second ch from hook; place marker to indicate the beginning of the rnd.

Rnd 2: 2 Sc in each sc around: 12 sc.

Rnd 3: (2 sc in next sc, sc in next sc) around: 18 sc.

Rnds 4-7: Sc in each sc around.

Rnd 8: (Sc2tog, sc in next sc) around, stuffing piece as you work: 12 sc.

Rnd 9: Sc2tog around; slip st in next sc, finish off leaving a long end for sewing: 6 sts.

Stuff Head firmly. Thread yarn needle with long end and weave through remaining 6 sts; pull **tightly** to close and secure end; then sew to the Body.

ARMS, LEGS & TAIL
With color indicated, work same as Standing Bunny.

Assembly

With strong thread, sew a plastic ring approximately 3" (7.5 cm) above top of the Mountain. Sew the stem of the Leaf to the center of the Base of the Mountain, and sew the loop of the Acorn to the end of the Oak Leaf. Dividing the circumference of the Base of the Mountain in thirds, sew the top of the Head of the Standing Bunny approximately 9" (23 cm) from the base. Sew the Grey Bunny at the back of the Head and Body approximately 9" (23 cm) from the Base and the White Bunny approximately 13" (33 cm) from the base.

GARLAND

Small Mountain

Rnd 1 (Right side)**:** With Grey, ch 3, 4 hdc in third ch from hook; place marker to indicate the beginning of the rnd.

Rnd 2: (2 Hdc in next hdc, hdc in next hdc) twice: 6 hdc.

Rnd 3: (2 Hdc in next hdc, hdc in next 2 hdc) twice: 8 hdc.

Rnd 4: (2 Hdc in next hdc, hdc in next 3 hdc) twice: 10 hdc.

Rnd 5: (2 Hdc in next hdc, hdc in next 4 hdc) twice: 12 hdc.

Rnd 6: (2 Hdc in next hdc, hdc in next 5 hdc) twice: 14 hdc.

Rnd 7: (2 Hdc in next hdc, hdc in next 6 hdc) twice: 16 hdc.

Rnd 8: (2 Hdc in next hdc, hdc in next 7 hdc) twice: 18 hdc.

Rnd 9: (2 Hdc in next hdc, hdc in next 8 hdc) twice: 20 hdc.

Rnd 10: (2 Hdc in next hdc, hdc in next 9 hdc) twice: 22 hdc.

Rnd 11: (2 Hdc in next hdc, hdc in next 10 hdc) twice: 24 hdc.

Rnd 12: (2 Hdc in next hdc, hdc in next 11 hdc) twice: 26 hdc.

Rnd 13: (2 Hdc in next hdc, hdc in next 12 hdc) twice; slip st in next hdc, finish off leaving a long end for sewing: 28 sts.

Stuff Mountain with polyester fiberfill and, using long end, sew bottom seam across Row to close.

SNOW CAP

Rnd 1 (Right side)**:** With White, ch 2, 4 sc in second ch from hook; place marker to indicate the beginning of the rnd.

Rnd 2: (2 Sc in next sc, sc in next sc) twice: 6 sc.

Rnd 3: (2 Sc in next sc, sc in next 2 sc) twice: 8 sc.

Rnd 4: (2 Sc in next sc, sc in next 3 sc) twice: 10 sc.

Rnd 5: 2 Sc in next sc, sc in next 4 sc, 2 hdc in next sc, hdc in next 4 sc: 12 sts.

Rnd 6: 2 Sc in next sc, sc in next 5 sc, 2 hdc in next hdc, hdc in next 5 hdc: 14 sts.

Rnd 7: 2 Sc in next sc, sc in next 6 sc, 2 hdc in next hdc, hdc in next 4 hdc, sc in next 2 hdc: 16 sts.

Rnd 8: Sc in the next 2 sc, hdc in next sc, 2 dc in next sc, hdc in next sc, sc in next sc, slip st in next sc, sc in next sc, hdc in next 2 hdc, 2 dc in next hdc, hdc in next 2 hdc, sc in next 2 sts; slip st in next sc, finish off leaving a long end for sewing.

Arrange the Snow Cap on the top of the Mountain, and using the long end, sew to Mountain.

Acorn (Make 2)

Rnd 1 (Right side)**:** With Medium Brown, ch 2, 3 sc in second ch from hook; place marker to indicate the beginning of the rnd.

Rnd 2: 2 Sc in each sc around: 6 sc.

Rnd 3: 2 Sc in each sc around: 12 sc.

Rnd 4: (2 Sc in next sc, sc in next sc) around: 18 sc.

Rnds 5-11: Sc in each sc around.

Rnd 12: (Sc2tog, sc in next sc) around, stuffing piece as you work: 12 sc.

Rnd 13: Sc2tog around; slip st in next sc, finish off leaving a long end for sewing: 6 sts.

Stuff piece firmly. Thread yarn needle with long end and weave through remaining 6 sts; pull **tightly** to close and secure end.

ACORN CAP

Rnd 1 (Right side)**:** With Dk Brown, ch 2, 10 sc in second ch from hook; place marker to indicate the beginning of the rnd.

Rnd 2: 2 Sc in each sc around: 20 sc.

Rnd 3: (2 Sc in next sc, sc in next sc) around: 30 sc.

Rnd 4: Sc in each sc around.

Rnd 5: (Sc2tog, sc in next sc) around; slip st in next sc, finish off leaving a long end for sewing: 20 sts.

OAK LEAF

With Green, ch 12.

Row 1 (Right side)**:** Sc in second ch from hook and in next 9 chs, 6 sc in last ch; working in free loops on opposite side of ch, sc in next 10 chs: 26 sc.

Row 2: Ch 1, turn; sc in first sc, ★ hdc in next sc, (dc, ch 3, slip st) in next sc, slip st in next sc, sc in next sc; repeat from ★ 2 times **more**, 2 hdc in same st as last sc, (2 hdc, sc) in next sc, † slip st in next sc, (slip st, ch 3, dc) in next sc, hdc in next sc, sc in next sc †; repeat from † to † 2 times **more**, slip st in first sc, ch 4 (for stem); finish off.

Work Stem on one Leaf ONLY.

ASSEMBLY

Arrange Acorn Cap on top of Acorn and with long end, sew Cap to Acorn. Make a ½" (12 mm) loop on the top of the Cap to form the stem.
Sew Oak Leaf to back of Acorn.

Large Crochet Bead (Make one **each** in the following colors: Medium Brown, Dk Brown, Lt Grey, Grey, Green & White)

Rnd 1 (Right side)**:** With color indicated, ch 2, 6 sc in second ch from hook; place marker to indicate the beginning of the rnd.

Rnd 2: 2 Sc in each sc around: 12 sc.

Rnd 3: (2 Sc in next sc, sc in next sc) around: 18 sc.

Rnds 4-7: Sc in each sc around.

Rnd 8: (Sc2tog, sc in next sc) around, stuffing piece as you work: 12 sc.

Rnd 9: Sc2tog around; slip st in next sc, finish off leaving a long end for sewing: 6 sts.

Stuff piece firmly. Thread yarn needle with long end and weave through remaining 6 sts; pull **tightly** to close and secure end.

Small Crochet Beads (Make one **each** in the following colors: Medium Brown, Dk Brown, Lt Grey, Grey, Green & White)

Rnd 1 (Right side)**:** With color indicated, ch 2, 6 sc in second ch from hook; place marker to indicate the beginning of the rnd.

Rnd 2: 2 Sc in each sc around: 12 sc.

Rnds 3-5: Sc in each sc around, stuffing piece as you work.

Rnd 6: Sc2tog around; slip st in next sc, finish off leaving a long end for sewing: 6 sts.

Standing Bunny

Work same as Mobile, page 30, using White for Head & Body, Arms, Legs & Ears and Lt Grey for Tail.

Assembly

Using strong thread, make a 5" (12.5 cm) loop on one end and thread the pieces from **right** to **left** in the following order:
Large Grey bead, large wood bead, small Dk Brown bead, small wood bead, large White bead, small Green

bead, Small Mountain, small wood bead, large Medium Brown bead, large wood bead, Acorn with Oak Leaf, large wood bead, small Grey bead, small wood bead, Standing Bunny, small wood bead, small Lt Grey bead, large wood bead, Acorn with Oak Leaf, large wood bead, large Dk Brown bead, small wood bead, Small Mountain, small Medium Brown bead, large Lt Grey bead, small White bead, large wood bead, large Green bead. Make a 5" (12.5 cm) loop with strong thread at left end.

STROLLER TOY

Oak Leaf (Make 2)

With Green, ch 12.

Row 1 (Right side)**:** Sc in second ch from hook and in next 9 chs, 6 sc in last ch; working in free loops on opposite side of ch, sc in next 10 chs: 26 sc.

Row 2: Ch 1, turn; sc in first sc, ★ hdc in next sc, (dc, ch 3, slip st) in next sc, slip st in next sc, sc in next sc; repeat from ★ 2 times **more**, 2 hdc in same st as last sc, (2 hdc, sc) in next sc, † slip st in next sc, (slip st, ch 3, dc) in next sc, hdc in next sc, sc in next sc †; repeat from † to † 2 times **more**, slip st in first sc, ch 4 (for stem); finish off.

Large Crochet Bead

(Make one **each** in the following colors: Lt Grey & White)

Rnd 1 (Right side)**:** With color indicated, ch 2, 6 sc in second ch from hook; place marker to indicate the beginning of the rnd.

Rnd 2: 2 Sc in each sc around: 12 sc.

Rnd 3: (2 Sc in next sc, sc in next sc) around: 18 sc.

Rnds 4-7: Sc in each sc around.

Rnd 8: (Sc2tog, sc in next sc) around, stuffing piece as you work: 12 sc.

Rnd 9: Sc2tog around; slip st in next sc, finish off leaving a long end for sewing: 6 sts.

Stuff piece firmly. Thread yarn needle with long end and weave through remaining 6 sts; pull **tightly** to close and secure end.

Small Crochet Beads

(Make one **each** in the following colors: Dk Brown & Grey)

Rnd 1 (Right side)**:** With color indicated, ch 2, 6 sc in second ch from hook; place marker to indicate the beginning of the rnd.

Rnd 2: 2 Sc in each sc around: 12 sc.

Rnds 3-5: Sc in each sc around, stuffing piece as you work.

Rnd 6: Sc2tog around; slip st in next sc, finish off leaving a long end for sewing: 6 sts.

Laying Down Bunny

Work same as Mobile, page 31, using Medium Brown for Head & Body, Arms, Legs & Ears and White for Tail.

Assembly

To make the Stroller Toy, use strong thread and secure to the right side clip (badge or alligator); then thread the pieces from **right** to **left** in the following order:

Small Dk Brown bead, large wood bead, Oak Leaf, large Lt Grey bead, large wood bead, Laying Down Bunny, large wood bead, large White bead, Oak Leaf, large wood bead, small Grey bead; then secure thread to left side clip.

Optional: Reinforce toy by threading another thread though all pieces, securing ends to clips.

Designs by Amy Gaines.

RATTLE

GAUGE: 20 sc and 20 rows = 4" (10 cm)

Head

Rnd 1 (Right side)**:** With larger size hook and White, make an adjustable ring *(**Figs. 1a-d, page 58**)*; ch 1, 6 sc in ring; place marker to indicate the beginning of the rnd.

Rnd 2: 2 Sc in each sc around: 12 sc.

Rnd 3: (Sc in next sc, 2 sc in next sc) around: 18 sc.

Rnd 4: (Sc in next 2 sc, 2 sc in next sc) around: 24 sc.

Rnd 5: (Sc in next 3 sc, 2 sc in next sc) around: 30 sc.

Rnd 6: (Sc in next 4 sc, 2 sc in next sc) around: 36 sc.

Rnds 7-14: Sc in each sc around.

Rnd 15: (Sc2tog, sc in next 4 sc) around: 30 sc.

Rnd 16: (Sc2tog, sc in next 3 sc) around: 24 sc.

Rnd 17: (Sc2tog, sc in next 2 sc) around: 18 sc.

Rnd 18: (Sc2tog, sc in next sc) around; slip st in next sc, finish off leaving a long end for sewing: 12 sts.

Ears (Make 2)

Rnd 1 (Right side)**:** With larger size hook and White, make an adjustable ring; ch 1, 6 sc in ring; place marker to indicate the beginning of the rnd.

Rnd 2: (2 Sc in next sc, sc in next 2 sc) twice: 8 sc.

Rnd 3: (2 Sc in next sc, sc in next 3 sc) twice: 10 sc.

Rnd 4: (2 Sc in next sc, sc in next 4 sc) twice: 12 sc.

Rnd 5: (2 Sc in next sc, sc in next 5 sc) twice: 14 sc.

Rnds 6-14: Sc in each sc around.

Slip st in next sc, finish off leaving a long end for sewing.

Large Bow

(Make one White & one Green)
With larger size hook and color indicated, make an adjustable ring; (ch 4, 4 tr, ch 4, slip st) twice in ring; finish off leaving a long end for sewing.

With Green Bow on top of White Bow, wrap Green yarn end twice around center of Bow; secure ends.

Small Bow

With larger size hook and Green, make an adjustable ring; (ch 3, 3 dc, ch 3, slip st) twice in ring; finish off leaving a long end for sewing.

Wrap long end twice around center of Bow; secure end.

Ring Cover

With larger size hook and Dk Brown, ch 9.

Row 1 (Right side)**:** Sc in second ch from hook and in each ch across: 8 sc.

Rows 2-19: Ch 1, turn; sc in each sc across.

Finish off leaving a long end for sewing.

Wrapping piece around wooden ring and using long end, sew end of rows together.

Assembly

Thread yarn needle with long end from Head and weave through remaining 12 sts; pull **tightly** to close and secure end; sew Head to center of Ring Cover.

Using photo as a guide for placement:

- Sew Ears to Head.
- With Black, add satin stitch eyes and nose; add straight stitch mouth.
- Sew Small Bow to base of one Ear.
- Sew Large Bows to Bunny "neck".

TEETHING TOY

GAUGE: 20 sc and 20 rows = 4" (10 cm)

Ring Cover

With larger size hook and Dk Brown, ch 9.

Row 1 (Right side)**:** Sc in second ch from hook and in each ch across changing to White in last sc ***(Fig. 4a, page 59)***; drop Dk Brown: 8 sc.

Rows 2 and 3: Ch 1, turn; sc in each sc across; at end of Row 3, change to Dk Brown in last sc; drop White.

Rows 4 and 5: Ch 1, turn; sc in each sc across; at end of Row 5, change to White in last sc; drop Dk Brown.

Rows 6-20: Repeat Rows 2-5, 3 times; then repeat Rows 2-4 once **more**.

Cut White.

Row 21: Ch 1, turn; slip st in each sc across; finish off leaving a long end for sewing.

Wrapping piece around wooden ring and using long end, sew end of rows together.

Crochet Bead (Make one with White & one with Green)

Rnd 1 (Right side)**:** With smaller size hook and color indicated, make an adjustable ring; ch 1, 6 sc in ring; place marker to indicate the beginning of the rnd.

Rnd 2: 2 Sc in each sc around: 12 sc.

Rnd 3: (Sc in next 2 sc, 2 sc in next sc) around: 16 sc.

Rnds 4 and 5: Sc in each sc around.

Insert wooden bead.

Rnd 6: (Sc2tog, sc in next 2 sc) around: 12 sc.

Rnd 7: (Sc2tog, sc in next sc) around: 8 sc.

Rnd 8: Sc2tog around; slip st in next sc, finish off leaving a long end for sewing: 4 sts.

Thread yarn needle with long end and weave through remaining 4 sts; pull **tightly** to close and secure end.

Assembly

Thread yarn needle with strong thread and add beads as follows: Geometric wood bead, small wood bead, small wood ring, small wood bead, Green crochet bead, small wood bead, alphabet beads spelling B A B Y, small wood bead, White crochet bead, small wood bead, small wood ring, small wood bead; then tie ends in a knot with beads around the striped ring cover.

Designs by Lisa Gentry.

BABY

ELEPHANT CIRCUS BABY SET

BABY

EASY

Finished Measurements:

Mobile - 23" (58.5 cm) tall

Garland - 54" (137 cm) long

Stroller Toy - 10" (25.5 cm) long

Rattle - 7" (18 cm) long (ring to ring) and 4½" (11.5 cm) wide (from trunk to back of head)

Teething Toy - 4" (10 cm) wide

SHOPPING LIST

Yarn (Medium Weight)

[4 ounces, 212 yards (113 grams, 194 meters) per skein]:

- ☐ Lt Grey - 1 skein

[5 ounces, 256 yards (141 grams, 234 meters) per skein]:

- ☐ White - 1 skein
- ☐ Red - 1 skein
- ☐ Black - small amount

Crochet Hook

- ☐ Size G (4 mm)

Additional Supplies

- ☐ Stitch marker
- ☐ Ring for Mobile
- ☐ 2¼" (5.5 cm) Wooden ring - 2
- ☐ 1¼" (3.25 cm) Wooden ring - 1
- ☐ Badge clip or alligator clip
- ☐ Large bell or plastic ball cat toy (for Rattle)
- ☐ Alphabet beads
- ☐ Yarn needle
- ☐ Polyester fiberfill
- ☐ Strong matching thread (for assembly)

STITCH GUIDE

SINGLE CROCHET 2 TOGETHER *(abbreviated sc2tog)*

Pull up a loop in each of next 2 sts, YO and draw through all 3 loops on hook **(counts as one sc)**.

MOBILE

Circus Tent

TRIANGLE (Make 3 Red and 3 White)

Row 1: With color indicated, ch 2, sc in second ch from hook: one sc.

Row 2: Ch 1, turn; 2 sc in sc: 2 sc.

Row 3: Ch 1, turn; 2 sc in first sc, sc in last sc: 3 sc.

Row 4: Ch 1, turn; 2 sc in first sc, sc in last 2 sc: 4 sc.

Row 5: Ch 1, turn; sc in each sc across.

Rows 6 and 7: Ch 1, turn; 2 sc in first sc, sc in each sc across: 6 sc.

Row 8: Ch 1, turn; sc in each sc across.

Rows 9 and 10: Ch 1, turn; 2 sc in first sc, sc in each sc across: 8 sc.

Row 11: Ch 1, turn; sc in each sc across.

Rows 12 and 13: Ch 1, turn; 2 sc in first sc, sc in each sc across: 10 sc.

Row 14: Ch 1, turn; sc in each sc across.

Rows 15 and 16: Ch 1, turn; 2 sc in first sc, sc in each sc across: 12 sc.

Row 17: Ch 1, turn; sc in each sc across.

Rows 18 and 19: Ch 1, turn; 2 sc in first sc, sc in each sc across: 14 sc.

Finish off.

BASE

Rnd 1 (Right side)**:** With Red, ch 2, 6 sc in second ch from hook; place marker to indicate the beginning of the rnd ***(see Markers, page 57)***.

Rnd 2: 2 Sc in each sc around: 12 sc.

Rnd 3: (2 Sc in next sc, sc in next sc) around: 18 sc.

Rnd 4: (2 Sc in next sc, sc in next 2 sc) around: 24 sc.

Rnd 5: (2 Sc in next sc, sc in next 3 sc) around: 30 sc.

Rnd 6: (2 Sc in next sc, sc in next 4 sc) around: 36 sc.

Rnd 7: (2 Sc in next sc, sc in next 5 sc) around: 42 sc.

Rnd 8: (2 Sc in next sc, sc in next 6 sc) around: 48 sc.

Rnd 9: (2 Sc in next sc, sc in next 7 sc) around: 54 sc.

Rnd 10: (2 Sc in next sc, sc in next 8 sc) around: 60 sc.

Rnd 11: (2 Sc in next sc, sc in next 9 sc) around: 66 sc.

Rnd 12: (2 Sc in next sc, sc in next 10 sc) around: 72 sc.

Rnd 13: (2 Sc in next sc, sc in next 11 sc) around: 78 sc.

Rnd 14: (2 Sc in next sc, sc in next 12 sc) around: 84 sc.

Rnd 15: Working in Back Loops Only ***(Fig. 3, page 59)***, sc in next sc, hdc in next 3 sc, (sc in next 3 sc, hdc in next 3 sc) 13 times, sc in next 2 sc.

Rnd 16: Working in both loops, sc in next sc, hdc in next 3 hdc, (sc in next 3 sc, hdc in next 3 hdc) 13 times, sc in next 2 sc.

Rnd 17: ★ Sc in next sc, hdc in next hdc, dc in next hdc, hdc in next hdc, sc in next sc, slip st in next sc; repeat from ★ around; slip st in next sc, finish off.

ASSEMBLY

Arrange the triangles with the last rows as the outside circumference of the circle (beginning ch in the center) alternating the colors (circumference with have a total of 84 sc). Sew the triangles together to form the tent. Stuff the top of the tent and arrange the tent on top of the right side of the Base at the unworked loops of Rnd 15 (84 sc total). Working through Back Loop on Triangle and free loop on Base, join Red with sc in any st ***(see Joining With Sc, page 57)***; sc in each st around in same manner; join with slip st to first sc, finish off.

With strong thread, sew a ring 4" (10 cm) from the center top of the Tent.

Elephant (Make 3)

HEAD AND BODY

Rnd 1 (Right side)**:** Starting at trunk with Grey, ch 2, 8 sc in second ch from hook; place a marker to indicate the beginning of the rnd.

Rnds 2-6: Sc2tog, sc in next sc, 2 sc in each of the next 2 sc, sc in next sc, sc2tog.

Rnd 7: Sc in next 2 sc, 2 hdc in each of the next 4 sc (top of the Head), begin stuffing the Trunk making sure it curves up to this point, sc in next 2 sc: 12 sts.

Rnd 8: Sc2tog, 2 hdc in each of next 8 hdc, sc2tog: 18 sts.

Rnd 9: Sc2tog, sc in next hdc, (2 hdc in next hdc, hdc in next hdc) 6 times, sc in next hdc, sc2tog: 22 sts.

Rnd 10: Sc2tog, (2 hdc in next hdc, hdc in next 2 hdc) 6 times, sc2tog: 26 sts.

Rnd 11: Sc2tog, sc in next 22 hdc, sc2tog: 24 sc.

Rnds 12-18: Sc in each sc around, stuffing Body firmly as you work.

Rnd 19: (Sc2tog, sc in next sc) around: 16 sc.

Rnd 20: Sc2tog around; slip st in next sc, finish off leaving a long end for sewing: 8 sts.

Stuff piece firmly. Thread yarn needle with long end and weave through remaining 8 sts ***(Fig. 5, page 60)***; pull **tightly** to close and secure end.

EAR (Make 2)

Row 1: With Grey, ch 2, 4 sc in second ch from hook.

Row 2: Ch 1, turn; 2 sc in each sc across: 8 sc.

Row 3: Ch 1, turn; 2 sc in the first sc, sc in next sc, (2 hdc in the next sc, hdc in next sc) twice, sc in next sc, 2 sc in last sc: 12 sts.

Row 4: Ch 1, turn; 2 sc in first sc, sc in next 2 sc, (2 hdc in the next hdc, hdc in next 2 hdc) twice, sc in next 2 sc, 2 sc in last sc; finish off leaving a long end for sewing: 16 sts.

FEET (Make 4)

Rnd 1 (Right side)**:** With Grey, ch 2, 8 sc in second ch from hook; place marker to indicate the beginning of the rnd.

Rnds 2-4: Sc in each sc around; at end of Rnd 4, slip st in next sc, finish off leaving a long end for sewing.

TAIL

With Grey, ch 5; cut yarn and pull end through ch on hook to finish off. Trim end approximately ½" (12 mm) from end and fray; this will be the end of the tail.

ASSEMBLY

Using photo as a guide for placement and referring to Embroidery Stitches, page 60:

- Sew Ears to sides of the Head.
- On 2 of the Elephants, fold the top of the ear down and towards the trunk and sew in place.
- Stuff Legs lightly and sew to bottom of Body.
- Sew Tail to rear of Body.
- With Black, embroider the eyes on either sides of the trunk.
- With Red, embroider a mouth under the trunk.

Finishing

Using photo as a guide for placement and strong thread to attach Elephants securely to the Bottom of the Tent:

Sew one Elephant with folded Ears approximately 12" (30.5 cm) from Bottom of the Tent.

Sew one Elephant without folded Ears approximately 8" (20.5 cm) from Bottom of the Tent.

Sew last Elephant with folded Ears approximately 4" (10 cm) from Bottom of the Tent.

GARLAND

Triangle (Make 7 Red and 8 White)

Row 1: With color indicated, ch 2, sc in second ch from hook: one sc.

Row 2: Ch 1, turn; 2 sc in sc: 2 sc.

Row 3: Ch 1, turn; 2 sc in first sc, sc in last sc: 3 sc.

Row 4: Ch 1, turn; 2 sc in first sc, sc in last 2 sc: 4 sc.

Row 5: Ch 1, turn; sc in each sc across.

Rows 6 and 7: Ch 1, turn; 2 sc in first sc, sc in each sc across: 6 sc.

Row 8: Ch 1, turn; sc in each sc across.

Rows 9 and 10: Ch 1, turn; 2 sc in first sc, sc in each sc across: 8 sc.

Row 11: Ch 1, turn; sc in each sc across.

Rows 12 and 13: Ch 1, turn; 2 sc in first sc, sc in each sc across: 10 sc.

Edging (Right side)**:** Ch 1, do **not** turn; work 12 sc evenly spaced across end of rows to beginning ch; (sc, ch 1, sc) in free loop of beginning ch ***(Fig. 2, page 59)***; work 12 sc evenly spaced across end of rows; working in sc across Row 13, (sc, ch 1, sc) in first sc, sc in next 8 sc, (sc, ch 1, sc) in last sc; join with slip st to first sc, finish off.

Weave in all yarn ends.

Crochet Bead (Make 2)

Rnd 1 (Right side)**:** With Grey, ch 2, 6 sc in second ch from hook; place marker to indicate the beginning of the rnd.

Rnd 2: 2 Sc in each sc around: 12 sc.

Rnds 3-5: Sc in each sc around, stuffing Bead as you work.

Rnd 6: Sc2tog around; slip st in next sc, finish off leaving a long end for sewing: 6 sc.

Stuff piece firmly. Thread yarn needle with long end and weave through remaining 6 sts; pull **tightly** to close and secure end.

Finishing

Using a long strand of strong thread:

- Secure and tie a 3" (7.5 cm) loop at one end.
- Run opposite end of thread through one Bead.
- Sew across the top of a white Triangle, then across the top of a red triangle. Continue sewing across the top of the Triangles, alternating colors.
- Run thread through last Bead.
- Secure and tie a 3" (7.5 cm) loop at opposite end.

STROLLER TOY

Large Crochet Bead

Rnd 1 (Right side)**:** With White, ch 2, 6 sc in second ch from hook; place marker to indicate the beginning of the rnd.

Rnd 2: 2 Sc in each sc around: 12 sc.

Rnd 3: (2 Sc in next sc, sc in next sc) around: 18 sc.

Rnds 4-7: Sc in each sc around, stuffing Bead as you work.

Rnd 8: (Sc2tog, sc in next sc) around: 12 sc.

Rnd 9: Sc2tog around; slip st in next sc, finish off leaving a long end for sewing: 6 sts.

Stuff piece firmly. Thread yarn needle with long end and weave through remaining 6 sts; pull **tightly** to close and secure end.

Small Crochet Bead (Make 2 Red and one White)

Rnd 1 (Right side)**:** With color indicated, ch 2, 6 sc in second ch from hook; place marker to indicate the beginning of the rnd.

Rnd 2: 2 Sc in each sc around: 12 sc.

Rnds 3–5: Sc in each sc around, stuffing Bead as you work.

Rnd 6: Sc2tog around; slip st in next sc, finish off leaving a long end for sewing: 6 sts.

Stuff piece firmly. Thread yarn needle with long end and weave through remaining 6 sts; pull **tightly** to close and secure end.

Elephant

Make one Elephant, page 46.

Ring Cover

With Red, ch 13.

Row 1: Sc in second ch from hook and in each ch across: 12 sc.

Rows 2-6: Ch 1, turn; sc in each sc across: 12 sc.

Finish off leaving a long end for sewing.

Wrap Ear Cover around 1¼" (3.25 cm) wooden ring; using long end, sew top of last row to base of beginning ch.

Finishing

Using photo as a guide for placement:
With strong thread, sew Small White bead to the center of the ring cover.
Sew Elephant to top of Small White bead.
Sew one Small Red bead to top of Elephant head.
Sew Large bead to Small White bead.
Sew last Small Red bead to Large bead.
Sew one ID or badge clip to top of last bead.

BABY

RATTLE

Elephant Head

Rnd 1 (Right side)**:** Starting at trunk with Grey, ch 2, 10 sc in second ch from hook; place marker to indicate the beginning of the rnd.

Rnds 2-8: Sc2tog, sc in next 2 sc, 2 sc in each of next 2 sc, sc in next 2 sc, sc2tog.

Rnd 9: Sc2tog, 2 hdc in each of next 6 sc (top of the Head), begin stuffing the Trunk making sure it curves up to this point, sc2tog: 14 sts.

Rnd 10: Sc2tog, 2 hdc in each of next 10 hdc, sc2tog: 22 sts.

Rnd 11: Sc2tog, sc in next 3 hdc, (2 hdc in next hdc, hdc in next hdc) 6 times, sc in next 3 hdc, sc2tog: 26 sts.

Rnd 12: Sc2tog, sc in next 2 sc, (2 hdc in next hdc, hdc in next 2 hdc) 6 times, sc the next 2 sc, sc2tog: 30 sts.

Rnds 13-18: Sc in each sc around, stuffing Head firmly as you work, inserting large bell or cat toy in the center.

Rnd 19: (Sc2tog, sc in next 3 sc) around: 24 sc.

Rnd 20: (Sc2tog, sc in next 2 sc) around: 18 sc.

Rnd 21: (Sc2tog, sc in next sc) around: 12 sc.

Rnd 22: Sc2tog around; slip st in next sc, finish off leaving a long end for sewing: 6 sts.

Stuff piece firmly. Thread yarn needle with long end and weave through remaining 6 sts; pull **tightly** to close and secure end.

Ear Cover (Make 2)

With Grey, ch 13.

Row 1: Sc in second ch from hook and in each ch across: 12 sc.

Rows 2-6: Ch 1, turn; sc in each sc across.

Finish off leaving a long end for sewing.

Wrap Ear Cover around 2¼" (5.5 cm) wooden ring; using long end, sew top of last row to base of beginning ch.

Finishing

Using photo as a guide for placement:

- Sew rings to each side of Head.
- With Black, add French knot eyes *(see Embroidery Sts, pages 60 & 61)*.
- With Red, embroider the mouth.

TEETHING TOY

Crochet Bead (Make 3 Grey and 2 **each** of White and Red)

Rnd 1 (Right side)**:** With color indicated, ch 2, 6 sc in second ch from hook; place marker to indicate the beginning of the rnd.

Rnd 2: 2 Sc in each sc around: 12 sc.

Rnds 3-5: Sc in each sc around, stuffing Bead as you work.

Rnd 6: Sc2tog around; slip st in next sc, finish off leaving a long end for sewing: 6 sts.

Stuff piece firmly. Thread yarn needle with long end and weave through remaining 6 sts; pull **tightly** to close and secure end.

Finishing

Using strong thread, string and secure beads in the following order: One Grey, one Red, one White, one Grey, one White, one Red, and one Grey bead. String alphabet beads spelling desired word; tie strong thread ends together.

Designs by Amy Gaines.

BABY

GENERAL INSTRUCTIONS

ABBREVIATIONS

ch(s)	chain(s)
cm	centimeters
dc	double crochet(s)
hdc	half double crochet(s)
mm	millimeters
Rnd(s)	Round(s)
sc	single crochet(s)
sc2tog	single crochet 2 together
st(s)	stitch(es)
tr	treble crochet(s)
YO	yarn over

SYMBOLS & TERMS

★ — work instructions following ★ as many **more** times as indicated in addition to the first time.

† to † — work all instructions from first † to second † **as many** times as specified.

( ) or [ ] — work enclosed instructions **as many** times as specified by the number immediately following **or** work all enclosed instructions in the stitch or space indicated **or** contains explanatory remarks.

colon — the number(s) given after a colon at the end of a row or round denotes the number of stitches or spaces you should have on that row or round.

Yarn Weight Symbol & Names	LACE 0	SUPER FINE 1	FINE 2	LIGHT 3	MEDIUM 4	BULKY 5	SUPER BULKY 6	JUMBO 7
Type of Yarns in Category	Fingering, size 10 crochet thread	Sock, Fingering, Baby	Sport, Baby	DK, Light Worsted	Worsted, Afghan, Aran	Chunky, Craft, Rug	Super Bulky, Roving	Jumbo, Roving
Crochet Gauge* Ranges in Single Crochet to 4" (10 cm)	32-42 sts**	21-32 sts	16-20 sts	12-17 sts	11-14 sts	8-11 sts	6-9 sts	5 sts and fewer
Advised Hook Size Range	Steel*** 6 to 8, Regular hook B-1	B-1 to E-4	E-4 to 7	7 to I-9	I-9 to K-10½	K-10½ to M/N-13	M/N-13 to Q	Q and larger

*GUIDELINES ONLY: The chart above reflects the most commonly used gauges and hook sizes for specific yarn categories.

** Lace weight yarns are usually crocheted with larger hooks to create lacy openwork patterns. Accordingly, a gauge range is difficult to determine. Always follow the gauge stated in your pattern.

*** Steel crochet hooks are sized differently from regular hooks–the higher the number, the smaller the hook, which is the reverse of regular hook sizing.

CROCHET TERMINOLOGY		
UNITED STATES		INTERNATIONAL
slip stitch (slip st)	=	single crochet (sc)
single crochet (sc)	=	double crochet (dc)
half double crochet (hdc)	=	half treble crochet (htr)
double crochet (dc)	=	treble crochet (tr)
treble crochet (tr)	=	double treble crochet (dtr)
double treble crochet (dtr)	=	triple treble crochet (ttr)
triple treble crochet (tr tr)	=	quadruple treble crochet (qtr)
skip	=	miss

GAUGE

Exact gauge is essential for proper fit. Before beginning your project, make a sample swatch in the yarn and hook specified. If your swatch is larger or smaller than specified, **make another, changing hook size to get the correct gauge.** Keep trying until you find the size hook that will give you the specified gauge.

MARKERS

Markers are used to help distinguish the beginning of each round being worked. Place a 2" (5 cm) scrap piece of yarn before the first stitch of each round, moving marker after each round is complete.

JOINING WITH SC

When instructed to join with sc, begin with a slip knot on hook. Insert hook in stitch or space indicated, YO and pull up a loop, YO and draw through both loops on hook.

BASIC	Projects using basic stitches. May include basic increases and decreases.
EASY	Projects may include simple stitch patterns, color work, and/or shaping.
INTERMEDIATE	Projects may include involved stitch patterns, color work, and/or shaping.
COMPLEX	Projects may include complex stitch patterns, color work, and/or shaping using a variety of techniques and stitches simultaneously.

CROCHET HOOKS																	
U.S.	B-1	C-2	D-3	E-4	F-5	G-6	7	H-8	I-9	J-10	K-10½	L-11	M/N-13	N/P-15	P/Q	Q	S
Metric - mm	2.25	2.75	3.25	3.5	3.75	4	4.5	5	5.5	6	6.5	8	9	10	15	16	19

ADJUSTABLE LOOP

Wind yarn around two fingers to form a ring *(Fig. 1a)*. Slide yarn off fingers and grasp the strands at the top of the ring *(Fig. 1b)*. Insert hook from **front** to **back** into the ring, pull up a loop, YO and draw through loop on hook to lock ring *(Fig. 1c)* (st made does **not** count as part of the beginning ch of the first rnd). Working around both strands, follow instructions to work sts in the ring, then pull yarn tail to close *(Fig. 1d)*.

Fig. 1a

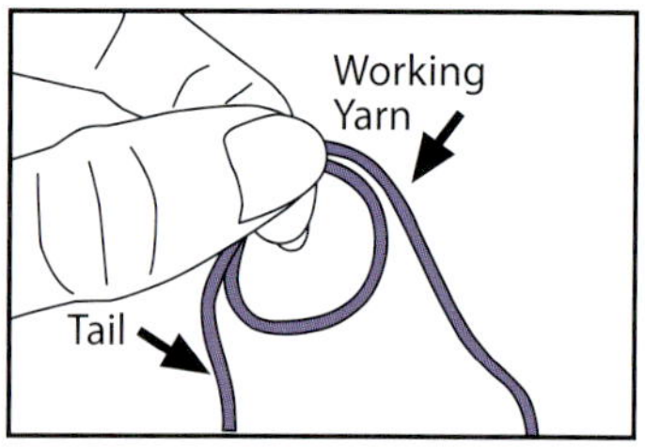

Fig. 1b

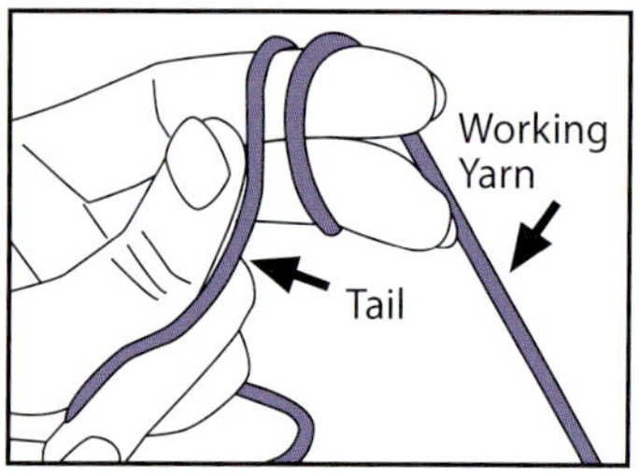

Fig. 1c

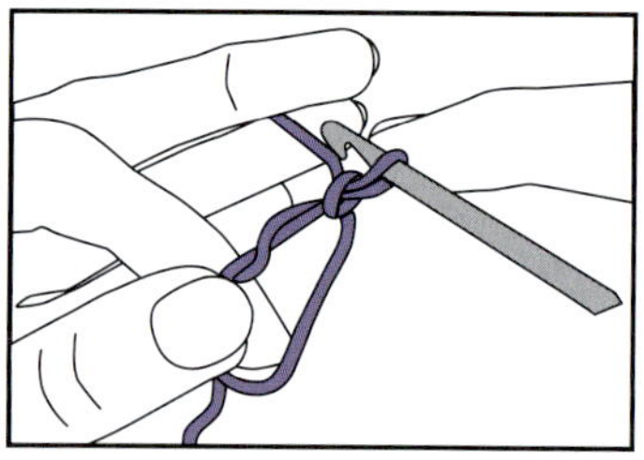

Fig. 1d

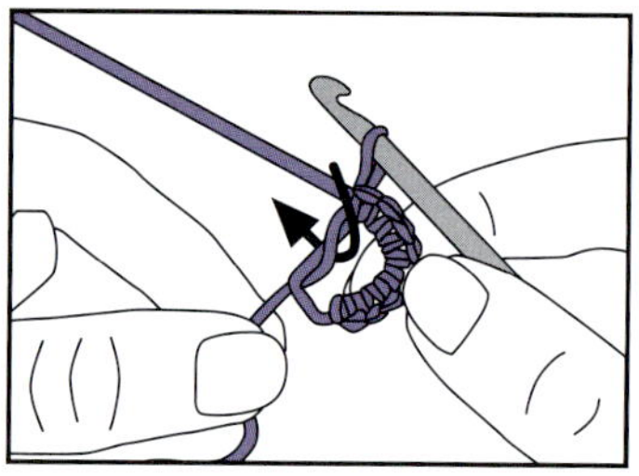

FREE LOOPS OF A CHAIN

When instructed to work in free loops of a chain, work in loop indicated by arrow *(Fig. 2)*.

Fig. 2

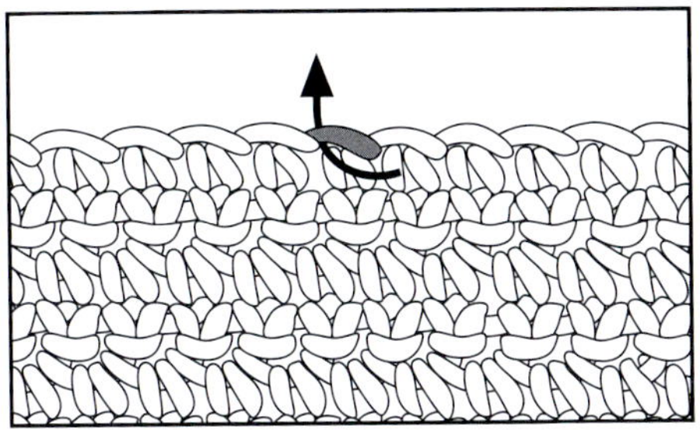

BACK OR FRONT LOOP ONLY

Work only in loop(s) indicated by arrow *(Fig. 3)*.

Fig. 3

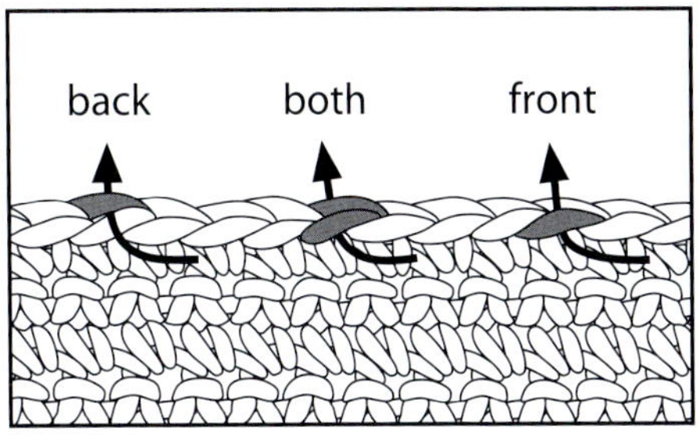

CHANGING COLORS

Work the last stitch to within one step of completion, hook new yarn *(Fig. 4a or b)* and draw through all loops on hook.

Fig. 4a

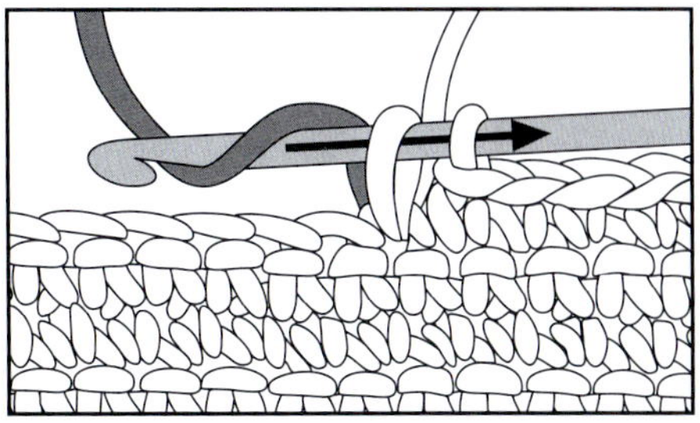

Fig. 4b

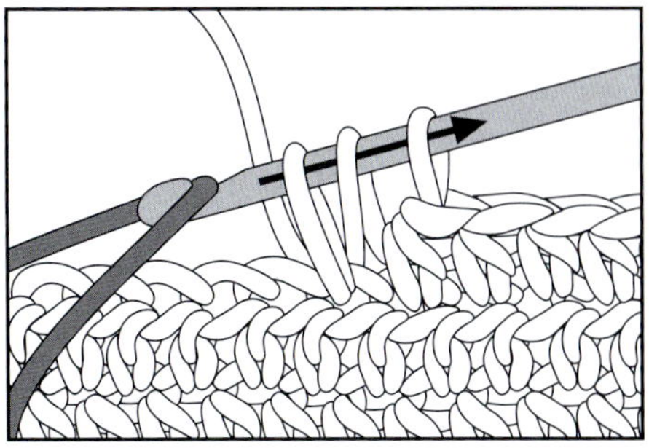

WEAVING THRU STITCHES

Weave yarn end through the stitches *(Fig. 5)* and gather to close.

Fig. 5

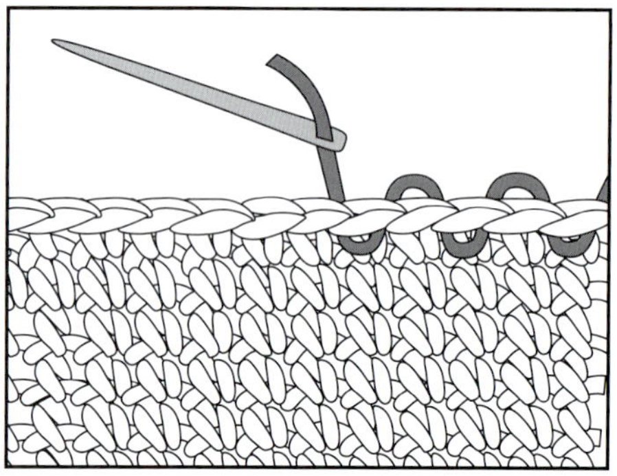

WHIPSTITCH

With **wrong** sides together, sew through both pieces once to secure the beginning of the seam. Insert the needle from **front** to **back** through **both** loops on **both** pieces *(Fig. 6)*. Bring the needle around and insert it from **front** to **back** through the next strand on **both** pieces. Continue in this manner keeping the sewing yarn fairly loose.

Fig. 6

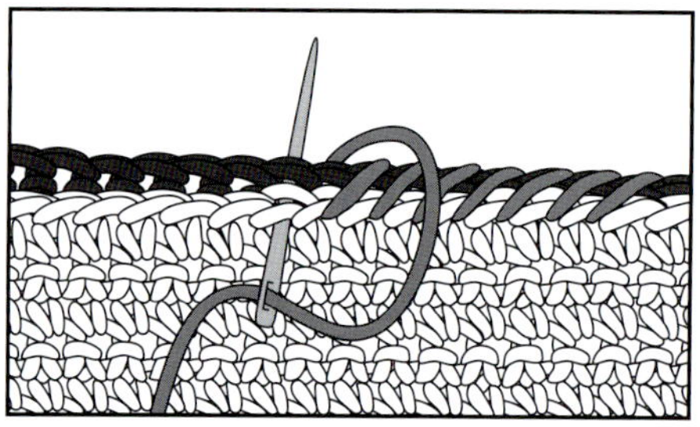

EMBROIDERY STITCHES

Backstitch

The backstitch is worked from **right** to **left**. Come up at 1, go down at 2 and come up at 3 *(Fig. 7)*. The second stitch is made by going down at 1 and coming up at 4.

Fig. 7

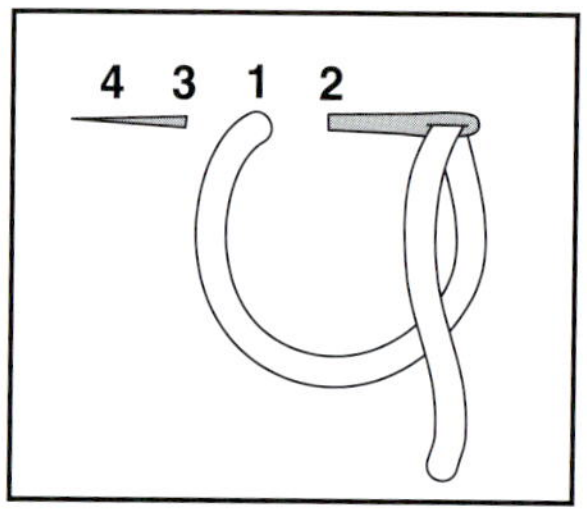

French Knot

Bring the needle up at 1. Wrap the yarn around the needle the desired number of times and insert needle at 2, holding end of yarn with non-stitching fingers ***(Fig. 8)***. Tighten knot; then pull needle through, holding yarn until it must be released.

Fig. 8

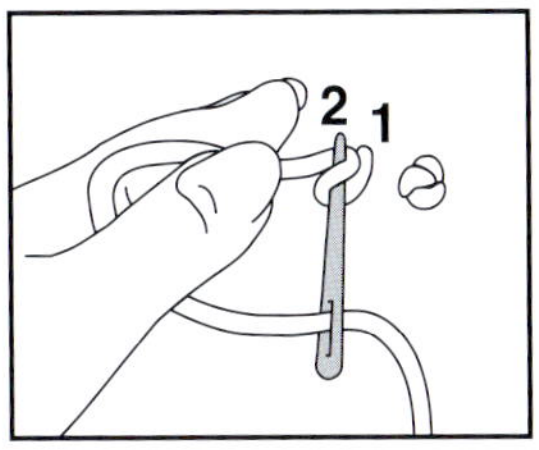

Satin Stitch

Satin stitch is a series of straight stitches worked side by side that come out of and go into the same stitch. Come up at odd numbers and go down at even numbers ***(Fig. 9)***.

Fig. 9

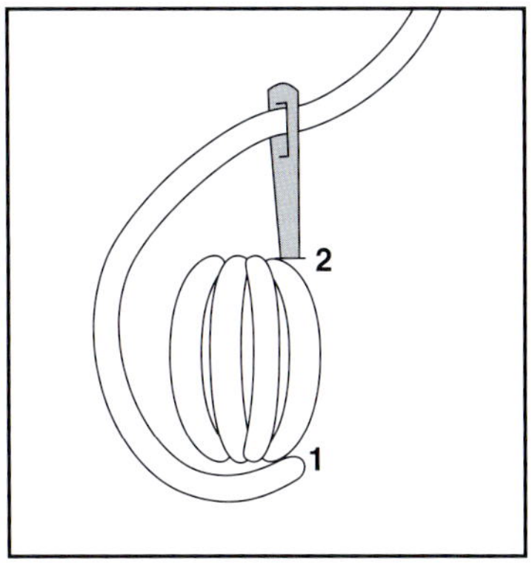

Straight Stitch

Straight stitch is just what the name implies, a single, straight stitch. Come up at 1and go down at 2 ***(Fig. 10)***.

Fig. 10

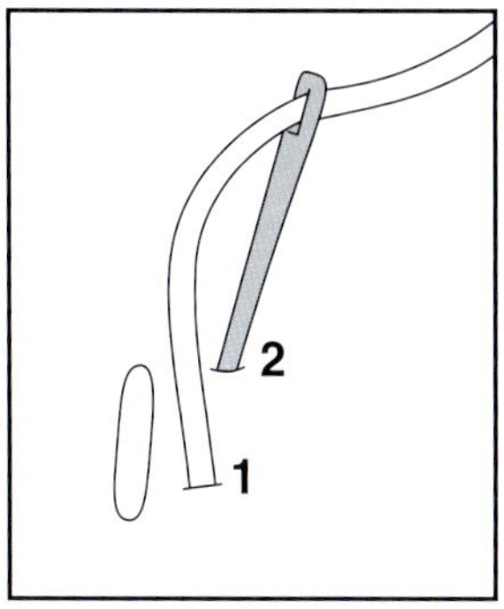

YARN INFORMATION

The projects in this book were made using a variety of Light Weight or Medium Weight yarn. Any brand of the specified weight may be used. It is best to refer to the yardage/meters when determining how many balls or skeins to purchase. Remember, to arrive at the finished size, it is the GAUGE/TENSION that is important, not the brand of yarn.

For your convenience, listed in the following column are the specific yarns and colors used to create out photography models. Because yarn manufacturers make frequent changes in their product lines, you may sometimes find it necessary to use a substitute yarn or to search for the discontinued product at alternate suppliers (locally or online).

BEEHIVE BABY SET

Bernat® Softee® Baby™

Gold - #54002 Buttercup

Grey - #30044 Flannel

Brown - #30010 Little Mouse

White - #02000 White

Yellow - #02003 Lemon

BUNNY BABY SET

Lion Brand® Vanna's Choice®

White - #100 White

Medium Brown - #125 Taupe

Dk Brown - #126 Chocolate

Green - #172 Kelly Green

Grey - #149 Silver Grey

Lt Grey - #150 Pale Grey

ELEPHANT CIRCUS BABY SET

Red Heart® Soft®

Lt Grey - #9440 Light Grey Heather

White - #4600 White

Red - #9925 Really Red

The Cataloging-in-Publication Data is on file with the Library of Congress.

We have made every effort to ensure that these instructions are accurate and complete. We cannot, however, be responsible for human error, typographical mistakes, or variations in individual work.

Production Team: Project Manager - Linda A. Daley; Graphic Artist - Angela Ormsby Stark; Photo Stylist - Lori Wenger; and Photographer - Jason Masters.

Made in U.S.A.